George Washington Carver

Betty Lou Kratoville

ORDER DIRECTLY FROM
ANN ARBOR PUBLISHERS LTD.
P.O. BOX 1, BELFORD
NORTHUMBERLAND NE70 7JX
TEL. 01668 214460 FAX 01668 214484
www.annarbor.co.uk

screams and the pounding of hooves.

Why would anyone take a young mother and her child? The answer was simple. Wicked men were getting rich by stealing slaves and selling them. No one had been able to stop them. Well, the Carvers would try!

Moses Carver hired a man to search for Mary and George. The man was gone for weeks. Then one day he walked in the front door of the Carver house. He was carrying a howling baby. It was George. The man had found him in a ditch! The kidnappers must have felt he was too much trouble and just tossed him away. The poor infant was more dead than alive.

Susan Carver took him in her arms. He

needed a bath. He needed clean clothes. He needed milk and food. In a short time he was clean and warm and asleep.

This was the beginning of George's good life with the Carvers. Mary was never heard of again.

Susan Carver stopped mixing cornbread. She looked George straight in the eye. "I wish you could, George. But the town charges a fee to go to that school. It's not much. But we don't have it."

George knew the Carvers would help him if they could. He also knew that he had to go to school. When he was ten, he thanked Moses and Susan Carver for all they had done. Then he said goodbye. He walked eight miles to Neosho. He had no money, no food, no extra clothes. He knew of no place to live.

The road was dusty. The sun was hot. When he got to Neosho, he saw a barn next door to the schoolhouse. He slept that night on a pile of hay in the barn. Early the next morning the owner of

George walked down a dusty road
toward a school in Neosho.

9

his sketches up over their fireplaces. From time to time he thought he might like to be an artist.

In the fall he headed for Highland College. He knew he had to sign up for classes. At the town pump he tidied himself up as best he could. It was at the college office that his world came tumbling down.

"We don't take Negroes here," said a clerk. "We never have, and we never will."

George stared at him. Then without a word he turned and left the office. What to do now? He had his savings for college. He would buy some land! He had heard that land was cheap in Ness County. And that is where he found some fields for sale. There was no house on the land. George didn't care. He built one himself of sod (chunks of soil held together by grass and its roots). It had only one small room. About this time he took Washington as a middle name.

George loved farming. He was not at all like the other farmers nearby. He would try one thing, then another. Some of his ideas worked. Some did not.

He was well liked by his neighbors. He talked to them about their crops. He often enjoyed a meal at their homes. He said thank you by drawing pictures for them.

In Ness County he had a much better life than at Fort Scott. He could have been very happy there. In fact, he *was* happy there. But – and it was a huge "but" – George could not forget about college. And then he heard about Simpson College in Iowa. A "For Sale" sign went up at once on George's land in Ness County.

CHAPTER 4

Time for a Change

Simpson College gave George a warm welcome. And they charged him a $12 fee. This left him with exactly 10 cents! Was he worried? Not George! He looked around and found an old empty shack. Just what he needed to set up a laundry business! All of the washing and ironing he had done through the years was now a great help. He began by washing his classmates' clothes. He soon had enough customers to eat three meals a day and to buy school books.

Now, what to study? George chose art. His teachers at Simpson felt he could be a fine artist. But George was not sure. Yes, he loved to draw and paint. But to spend a whole life drawing pretty pictures? He felt he had more to give to the world than that.

What about growing things? George knew that after the Civil War farmers in the South were in deep trouble. Once huge cotton crops had made them rich. Now cotton plants were brown and scrawny. What was wrong? There had to be a reason. George thought he might be helpful. But he felt he needed to know a lot more.

Then he heard about the Iowa State College of Agriculture. Agriculture! A big word that covered a lot. Everything to do with things that grew was taught there. George got himself into Iowa State just as fast as he could. Once there he took class after class. He learned about plant diseases. He learned how to "cross" one plant with another. He learned about worn-out soil. There was so much to learn. And he vowed to learn it all.

George graduated from Iowa State in 1894. His teachers there asked him to stay on. They needed someone to be head of the college greenhouses. It was the chance of a lifetime. George grabbed it. It meant he could keep on with his studies. It also felt good to stay with the many friends he had made.

It was about this time that George found a way to share his ideas. He spent his free hours writing pamphlets. In these he told farmers how to make their crops better. The little baby who had been thrown into a ditch was becoming well-known all over the country. Agriculture had found a new leader.

George most likely would have been happy to stay at Iowa State for the rest of his life. But then one day a letter came for him. It was from a man named Booker T. Washington. George knew that name. Years before, Booker T. Washington had started a school in Tuskegee, Alabama. It had only one goal. That was to teach free black people the skills they needed to earn a living.

Washington and his school were now quite famous.

His letter read:

I cannot offer you money or fame. I offer you in their place work – hard, hard work – the task of bringing people from poverty and waste to full manhood.

It did not take George long to make up his mind. Tuskegee was where he had to be!

CHAPTER 5

A New Post

George left for Tuskegee with high hopes. He had heard so much about Booker T. Washington. Surely Tuskegee would offer a chance to try out new ideas. His hopes sank as soon as he got there! He had thought there would be a lab with lots of supplies. He was shown an empty room. He had thought there would be a dairy. Instead he found just one cow. He had thought there would be a greenhouse. Wrong again!

What did he find? A few bare buildings.

Then he started to test the Alabama soil.

Hard-packed soil with nothing growing on it. Poor families with hungry children. Fields of dry, dusty cotton plants. It was clear that George had a lot of work to do.

Where to begin? First, he had to do something about a lab. The school had no money. George rounded up some students. "Let's see what we can find," he said.

People stared when they saw George and his students searching rubbish heaps for jars and bottles. They also found old pots and pans and bits of rubber. Somehow George was able to turn this junk into useful lab items. Then he started to test the Alabama soil. And it wasn't long before he got results.

The problem with the cotton crops was very simple. This is how George explained it to the poor farmers, both black and white: Cotton plants drain all the rich minerals out of the soil. After a few years the fields are useless for cotton. But farmers have kept on planting cotton because they didn't know what else to grow.

A lot of forests were burned by men seeking new land. But these new lands would last for only a few plantings of cotton. Then they, too, were no good.

What was the answer? George thought he had it: Make the soil rich again. But how does one do that? By planting crops that can put the minerals back in the soil.

George's first crop was 20 acres of cowpeas. His students thought their new teacher was slightly mad. No one ate cowpeas. They were fed to hogs.

"Just wait," said George with a smile. When the cowpeas were ripe, he picked them and turned them into a tasty meal.

"Now we will plant sweet potatoes in the same field," said George. This time his students said not a word. The sweet potato crop grew and grew.

"Now I will tell you what we have been doing," George told his students. "First we planted cowpeas. Then we planted sweet potatoes. Those two crops put the rich minerals back in the soil that cotton had used up. Now we can plant cotton again. This is called 'crop rotation.' All you are doing is giving your soil a rest."

People came from miles around to see George's cotton crop. No one had seen fluffy white cotton bolls like that for years. They looked at one another with new hope in their eyes.

They came for another reason, too. George had not forgot Mariah's skills with plants and herbs. He brewed teas from local plants and herbs. His brews seemed to ease people's pain and to heal their sores. Some people thought they had more pep after drinking his tea. These days we think that George's plants and herbs were full of vitamins. That may be why people felt so much better after they took them. At that time vitamins were unheard of – even by George. All he knew was that after using the herbs, people didn't hurt anymore. So he kept on gathering plants and drying them and giving them to his neighbors.

CHAPTER 6

The "Movable School"

Some farmers lived too far from George to seek his help. This worried him. Then one day he had a new thought. If people could not come to him, he would go to the people.

He found an old cheap wagon and a mule. He filled the wagon with farm tools and plants. His students called his wagon the "Movable School." Sometimes they went with him on his trips down the dusty country roads.

The farmers were always glad to see this

gentle man. He had so much to teach. They had so much to learn. He showed them what to use to make their crops grow better. He taught them how to prune their fruit trees. He canned and dried meats and vegetables in their kitchens. In this way their wives were able to put away food for the winter. Now and then someone would offer to pay him.

"No, thank you," he would say. "If I know the answer, you can have it for the price of a postage stamp. The Lord charges me nothing for knowledge, and I will charge you the same."

Soon his trips took him past fields of healthy white cotton plants. The people had listened to him. They had rotated their crops. It made George feel very good indeed!

Then disaster struck! The farmers woke up one morning and could not believe their eyes. All of the cotton buds had turned brown and fallen to the ground. The cotton plants had dried up. What had caused this? George Carver knew. It was the boll weevil. What in the world was a boll weevil? It was a little worm that had made its way from Mexico through the South. Now it had reached Alabama. What could be done? Nothing!

The poor farmers rushed to George. "Please help us," they begged.

"There is nothing I can do," he said. "You will have to plow up your fields of cotton. Then plant peanuts."

"Peanuts? What can we do with peanuts? They are only good for feeding animals," the farmers told him.

"You have no other choice," he said.

And so they planted peanuts. The peanut crops did well. In fact, everyone had barns full of peanuts. There was only one snag. No one wanted to buy them.

Once again the farmers went to George for help. And he went to his lab. He locked himself in for a week. When he came out, he had found two dozen new uses for the lowly peanut! Think of it! Cooking oil could be made from peanuts. And shampoo . . . and five kinds of breakfast cereal . . . even ice cream!

Then it was time to tell the world about the value of peanuts. George asked a group of businessmen for lunch. He gave his guests soup, bread, "chicken" loaf, ice cream, and cookies. The men enjoyed the meal. Then George told them that every single thing they had eaten had been made from peanuts. From then on, peanut sales did very well!

CHAPTER 7

Fame!

Now another welcome letter came for George. He was asked to speak at a meeting of a group of peanut growers. He packed a box full of things to show. Then he got on a bus for Montgomery. His speech was a great hit. It was hard to believe how many things could be made from peanuts: cheese, dyes, peanut butter, paper, ink. People stood up and cheered.

"I think Professor Carver should go to Washington," said one man. "He needs to spread the word about peanuts." George did not like to leave his home and lab. But he said he would do this.

On January 21, 1921, he climbed the steps of the U.S. Capitol. He carried his heavy box of samples. He had been told that he would have 15 minutes to speak. At first no one seemed to care much about what he had to say. Then slowly the great hall grew quiet. Two hours went by before the Congressmen let him go.

Newspapers heard of George's work. They printed stories about his talk to Congress. Their readers were surprised. How useful was the peanut! By this time George had found even more ways to use the peanut. The news stories told for young people of every race. His grave at Tuskegee has the following words:

HE COULD HAVE ADDED FORTUNE

TO FAME, BUT CARING FOR

NEITHER, HE FOUND HAPPINESS

AND HONOR IN BEING HELPFUL TO

THE WORLD.